IMAGES
of America

HERBST DEPARTMENT STORE

ON THE COVER: Herbst's first Dollar Day Sale drew large crowds on May 23, 1923. For more information, see page 82. (Courtesy of the North Dakota State University Archives.)

IMAGES
of America

HERBST DEPARTMENT STORE

Trista Raezer and John Hallberg

ARCADIA PUBLISHING

ISBN 978-1-4671-1447-9

Published by Arcadia Publishing
Charleston, South Carolina

Printed in the United States of America

Library of Congress Control Number: 2015932701

For all general information, please contact Arcadia Publishing:
Telephone 843-853-2070
Fax 843-853-0044
E-mail sales@arcadiapublishing.com
For customer service and orders:
Toll-Free 1-888-313-2665

Visit us on the Internet at www.arcadiapublishing.com

We dedicate this book to the memory of Andrea Hunter Halgrimson, longtime supporter and friend of the NDSU Archives.

Contents

ACKNOWLEDGMENTS

The authors would like to express their deep appreciation to several individuals and organizations for their support and assistance with this book. First and foremost we would like to thank Bob Herbst for donating the collection to the NDSU Archives in 1986, and the interest and support from Bob, Edith, and the Herbst family in allowing us to share their family's story. We would also like to thank Byron Bergman for providing a perspective on the store that only a longtime employee could provide, as well as allowing us to use several of his photographs. Much appreciation also goes to Andrea Hunter Halgrimson for allowing us to use the Herbst clipping file from the *Forum* newspaper library; this book would have been nearly impossible to write without it. Thanks also go to the staff at the Fargo-Moorhead Community Theater for allowing us to peruse their photographs for an image of the Emma K. Herbst Playhouse. Lastly, thanks also go to Scherling Photography for giving permission to publish several photographs attributed to their studio.

Unless otherwise noted, all images appear courtesy of the North Dakota State University Archives.

INTRODUCTION

The history of the Herbst Department Store closely parallels that of Fargo, North Dakota. In 1887, a young man from Cincinnati, Ohio, arrived in the young city of Fargo. Isaac "Ike" Herbst had learned the clothing business in Cincinnati and was ready to ply his trade in the newly tamed West. After a few years working for others, he went into partnership with Robert Adler to buy out the stock of a bankrupt business, and they sold out in two months. The pair then went into purchasing and selling wholesale goods from New York and met with great success. In 1892 Herbst had enough money to buy out his partner, and his store was founded.

Emma Krohn came to Fargo in 1892 from Freeport, Illinois, to visit her cousins, the wives of Alex and Max Stern. The Sterns happened to have a store next door to Herbst, and in December Emma Krohn and Ike Herbst married. This proved to be a fortuitous match that resulted in two sons, Krohn Herbst and Robert K. Herbst. Fargo and the young couple soon faced one of the worst disasters either would experience. On June 7, 1893, a fire broke out in Herzman's Dry Goods Store and burned down 31 blocks of downtown Fargo before the day was through. Among the 219 businesses destroyed was Herbst's. Neither Fargo nor Herbst were daunted, and both rebuilt. The store reopened at 56 Broadway on October 14, 1893. When his rebuilt store caught on fire a few months later, Herbst still did not give up.

In 1898, the store arrived at its final location, at 16 Broadway. Herbst was beyond successful and perhaps the first businessman in Fargo to feature merchandise in display windows. Unfortunately, Herbst passed away unexpectedly in 1910 at the age of 51. The store and a $50,000 fortune went to his widow. Emma Herbst took a firm hold of the reins and ushered the store into a new era of prosperity and progress. As president, she continued the expansion of the store and paved the way for her son Krohn to take over when he was old enough. She served the growing Fargo community by not only presiding over a popular downtown establishment but by serving on school boards, in the Red Cross, and as a board trustee of the National Tuberculosis Society. She stepped down to the role of vice president and treasurer when Krohn took over as president in 1919.

Emma did not slow down with her work for the store. She cared deeply for the employees and started the Social and Benefit Club, also known as the S&B Club, shortly after Christmas in 1920. She donated $500 to the club, and one percent of employees' salaries went into the club treasury. The store matched each dollar in full. The club, run by employees, provided entertainment at various times of the year, sick benefits, death benefits, flowers for the sick, and charitable donations. The club proved to be popular and existed until the store went out of business in 1982. Sadly, Emma Herbst did not live long enough to see the results of her son's largest achievement, a complete remodel and expansion of the store, which added two stories and 48,000 square feet. She at least got to see the new façade before she passed away in 1925, leaving behind an estate worth $363,000. Before passing on, she said that building the new store was "a manifestation of faith in Fargo and the Northwest."

Krohn Herbst was as astute a businessperson as his parents. He brought on his younger brother, Robert K., as vice president and treasurer. Krohn loved to travel, and filled his office at the store and his apartment with opulent treasures bought on his trips. He traveled to New York City for buying trips quite often to ensure that the citizens of Fargo had access to the latest fashions. Unfortunately, Krohn passed away at the age of 40 in 1934 after an appendectomy.

Robert K. did not expect to become president of the Herbst Department Store so soon, but like his mother before him, he took to it immediately and continued leading the store down the road of progress. Under Robert K.'s direction, the store expanded exponentially. Among his many accomplishments were the addition of an electric neon sign in 1936, air-conditioning in 1954, the purchase of the adjacent Luger Furniture Store to the south in 1958, and a new parking lot behind the store in 1961. The only setback was a small warehouse fire set by an arsonist in 1950.

Like his older brother, Robert K. was a vital member of the growing Fargo community. He started a popular radio station in the 1930s, was a founding member of Temple Beth El in 1942, and served in the Navy during World War II. In 1964, he founded the Herbst Family Foundation to make gifts to educational, literary, religious, and scientific organizations.

Robert K. retired in 1965, allowing his three sons to take over the ever popular and growing store that was a vital part of Fargo's growing downtown. Robert B. "Bob" became president, Michael vice-president, and Richard "Dick" secretary-treasurer. The adjacent Edwards Building to the north was acquired in 1966. A new façade was built to cover the entire face of the store. This unified the buildings and gave a new and modern look to the store.

The 75th anniversary, in 1967, was a huge and spectacular event. The Herbst family made every anniversary special, but they went all out for the 75th. It was a many-weeks-long event, with huge sales and drawings, historical clothing for employees to wear, and a party that had three generations of Herbsts present. The mayor of Fargo, Hershel Lashkowitz, even signed a proclamation from the city celebrating the store and the family.

The 75th anniversary proved to be the swan song for Herbst's. In 1972, the West Acres Shopping Center was opened on the outskirts of Fargo, drawing shoppers away from downtown as malls did in most cities across America in the 1960s and 1970s. In 1974, yet another fire occurred, causing the store to close for a few months. The loss of revenue was hard to recover from, and many customers did not come back. The three brothers tried to keep the store going and even opened four branch stores across the state in Bismarck, Devils Lake, Jamestown, and at the West Acres Shopping Center, but it was not enough. Fargo's downtown was losing its popularity and stores to the mall. Each branch store closed, one after the other, and the main store closed for good in 1982, after 90 years of continuous operation.

While the Herbst story ended, Fargo's downtown re-blossomed in the mid-2000s. Dedicated citizens of Fargo missed the vibrant downtown of days past and worked to renovate and restore historic buildings, enticing small businesses to come back. The Herbst Department Store buildings still stand and have been restored to their original look. The store and family have not been forgotten, and we hope to keep that memory from fading.

One

The Herbst Family

Isaac "Ike" Herbst, patriarch of the Herbst family, was born in Cincinnati, Ohio, in 1858 to a German Jewish family. After learning the clothing trade, he moved to Dakota Territory in 1884, spending time in both Jamestown and Bismarck. He arrived in Fargo in 1887 and worked for B. & I. Sternberg Store and the Yerxa Company.

During the summer of 1892, 24-year-old Emma Krohn of Freeport, Illinois, came to Fargo to visit her cousins, who were married to the Stern brothers, Alex and Max. These two brothers happened to own a store that was next door to Ike Herbst's. On December 31, 1892, Ike and Emma married in Freeport.

The Herbst family home was built for Ike Herbst around 1897. It was located at 221 Eighth Street South, among the homes of other prominent Fargo families. After Ike and Emma died, the home remained in the family until about 1940. It was torn down around 1969 to make room for a parking lot.

On December 10, 1893, Ike and Emma Herbst's first son, Jacob Krohn Herbst, was born. He went by his middle name. He attended the high school at the North Dakota Agricultural College (now North Dakota State University) in Fargo for two years and graduated from the Northwestern Naval and Military Academy in Wisconsin. After his father passed away on June 21, 1910, Krohn worked at the store with his mother.

Krohn Herbst enlisted in the Army reserves in Chicago on October 19, 1917, and was called into active duty a few months later at Camp Joseph E. Johnson in Florida. He was discharged as a quartermaster sergeant on December 3, 1918. The following month, he took over as president of the Herbst Department Store. Emma remained active in the store by serving as vice president until her death on June 10, 1925.

Krohn Herbst inherited his parents' astute business skills. Ike left behind an estate valued at $50,000 upon his death, and Emma left behind an estate valued at $363,000 upon her death in 1925. When Krohn applied for a position in the civil service at age 23, he mentioned that he "had entire charge and management of the store, hiring and discharging of all employees, overseeing of all purchasing and inspection of all merchandise."

Krohn Herbst's office at the Herbst Department Store was opulently decorated with items he purchased on his many buying trips abroad. Krohn died unexpectedly at the age of 40 on November 28, 1934, during an appendectomy operation. He never married. Krohn's younger brother, Robert K., took over as president of the Herbst Department Store.

Ike and Emma Herbst's second son, Robert Krohn Herbst, was born on August 17, 1903. He graduated from the Northwestern Naval and Military Academy in Wisconsin in 1922 and from the University of Pennsylvania's prestigious Wharton School in 1926. He married Frances Burton and became the vice president of Herbst Department Store in 1926. He stayed in that position until his older brother passed away, whereupon he took over the store.

Robert K. Herbst (center, with captain's hat) was involved in many civic and philanthropic activities and was an avid world traveler. In 1937, he started the KVOX radio station in Moorhead, Minnesota, was a founding member of Temple Beth El in 1942, and served in the Navy as a lieutenant commander.

In 1964, Robert K. Herbst donated $25,000 to help furnish a new theater in Fargo's Island Park for the Fargo Moorhead Community Theatre group. It was originally called the Emma K. Herbst Playhouse in honor of his mother. The building still stands and is currently known as the Stage at Island Park. (Courtesy of the Fargo-Moorhead Community Theatre.)

Robert K. Herbst lived in this Tudor Revival home from 1939 to 1975. It is located at 901 Fourteenth Avenue South, and still stands to this day, looking very much the same. The home was built around 1929 for Harry E. Reynolds, manager of a wholesale fruits company.

Robert K. Herbst and his wife, Frances, had three sons, Robert B. "Bob," Michael, and Richard. Bob graduated from the Shattuck Military Academy in Faribault, Minnesota, in 1945, then spent two years in the Navy, received a business degree in 1949 from the University of Michigan in Ann Arbor, and married Edith Winter in 1955. They had three children, Susan, Nancy, and James.

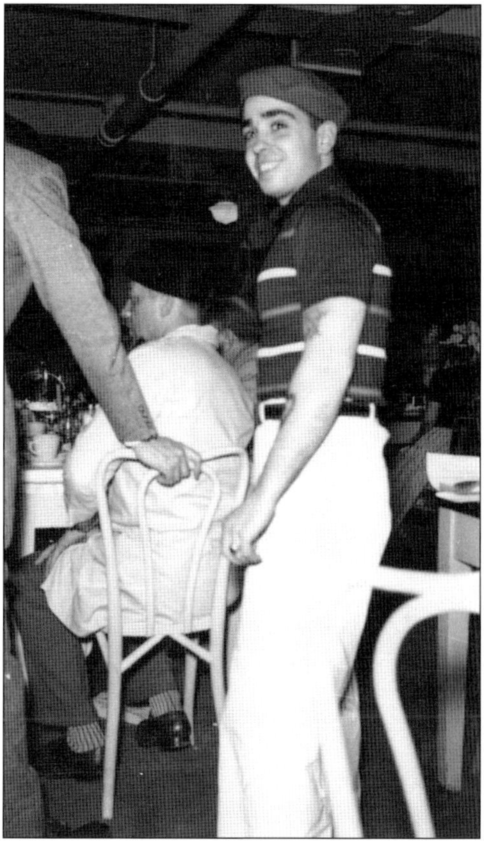

Bob Herbst became president and general manager upon his father's retirement in October 1965. His younger brothers, Michael and Richard, became vice president and secretary-treasurer respectively. Here Bob can be seen giving a retirement gift to longtime employee Hazel Sandsmark in 1967. He remained president of the Herbst Department Store until its closure in 1982. His father, Robert K., died the year before the store closed.

The three Herbst brothers dressed in late 19th century costume for the Herbst Department Store's 75th anniversary in 1967. They are, from left to right, Michael, Bob, and Richard. The three brothers were partners with their father in the Herbst Development Company.

Four of the Herbst family members can be seen here. From left to right are Frances Herbst, Robert K. Herbst, Bob Herbst, and his wife, Edith Herbst. Frances gathered over 300 dolls during her travels to 70 countries. She donated the dolls to the College of Home Economics at NDSU in 1974. (Courtesy of Byron Bergman.)

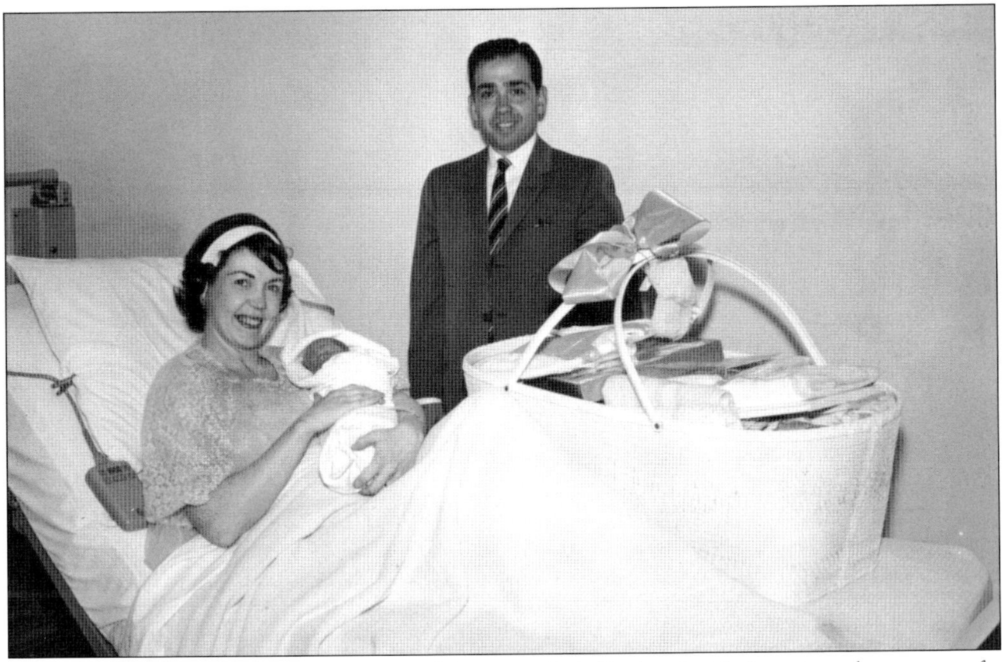

To help celebrate the 75th anniversary of the store, Bob Herbst decided to give a layette set of a bassinette, clothing, and other items for a newborn to the 75th baby born at the Dakota Hospital in Fargo. Randal Wraalstad, son of Joan Wraalstad, was the lucky winner.

Bob Herbst was extremely active in the Fargo community. He served as the president of Fargo's chamber of commerce, Fargo's downtown business association, Fargo Parking Authority, Temple Beth El, North Dakota State Retailers Association, and chairman of the Broadway Mall Committee. He was also involved with the Boy Scouts, Kiwanis, Jaycees, Elks Lodge, and the Fargo Country Club.

Michael, the middle brother (1930–1995), graduated from Fargo Central High School and North Dakota State University in 1953, and started working for the Herbst Department Store in 1959. He married Sheree Cornfeldt in 1954 and had three daughters, Barbara, Amy, and Caren. He later married Sheila Flemings. He served as the president of Temple Beth El and was involved with the Fargo Moorhead Community Theatre, the Tri-College University, United Way, the Lions Club, YMCA, Jaycees, Fargo Country Club, and Elks Lodge.

Richard Herbst (front row, fourth from the left) was the youngest of the three brothers. He graduated from Fargo Central High School and the University of Arizona, married Barbara Ingberg in 1962, and had three children, Kathryn, Stephen, and Lisa. He later married Susan Oliver. He was active in the Fargo community and served as the president of the Red River Valley Fair Association. Here he is pictured with the association board. He opened a bagel shop in the 1990s and worked for a time at NDSU.

Two

THE HERBST BUILDING

This photograph looking south on Broadway was taken during the Firemen's Tournament parade on July 12, 1889. It shows what Fargo looked like during Ike Herbst's first years in the city. The location of his first business, the Bankrupt Store, is visible in the distance just left of the building with "The Boston" sign painted on it.

The first store owned by Ike Herbst was destroyed in the Great Fargo Fire of June 7, 1893. This photograph taken during the height of the conflagration is looking east on Northern Pacific Avenue, near its intersection with Broadway. The Herbst store was located just north of the National Bank of Fargo building, the brick building visible at far left.

After the Great Fargo Fire of 1893, Ike Herbst and Company occupied the Citizens National Bank building, visible here shortly after construction. The store was L shaped with two entrances, one on Northern Pacific Avenue, visible with awning at left, and one on Broadway, visible behind the wagon at right.

Ike Herbst & Company's second store reopened for business at 56 Broadway on October 14, 1893. But, this new location was plagued by a second fire, which struck just a few months later on January 23, 1894. This time, the building was spared; however, all the merchandise was destroyed and the showroom heavily damaged. Herbst recovered from this setback and within several years outgrew this space.

In 1898, a new two-story building was constructed for what was now Herbst Department Store, located a block south at 16 Broadway. The grand opening took place on September 1 of that year. Ike Herbst is pictured here standing beside his horse-drawn buggy, parked in front of the new store building. (Courtesy of Bob Herbst.)

This elevated view looking north on Broadway features the store building as it appeared in 1909. It is just to the right of the Luger Furniture building, visible at far left. A trolley system, seen here, brought customers into downtown from the surrounding neighborhoods.

This postcard image from 1909 is looking south on Broadway from its intersection with Northern Pacific Avenue. The Herbst Department Store is on the right. At the time this photograph was taken, the cities of Fargo and Moorhead had a population of nearly 20,000. This bustling street scene is evidence that the cities were the commercial hub for a much broader population in the surrounding agricultural communities.

In this 1915 view of the showroom, a cable wire is running across the room. This was part of a mechanical cash system. The sales clerks on the floor would make a sale and send the payment in a basket to a cashier in a separate room. The cashier would then process the transaction and send the change and receipt back to the customer.

A crowd of Christmas shoppers brave the winter weather in front of the Herbst Department Store during the Dollar Day Sale of December 2, 1922. According to an advertisement, this promotional event was held every 90 days and had a history of attracting about 35,000 people. With the booming business, there came a need for more space.

On September 8, 1922, plans for a major building expansion were announced. Groundbreaking took place in July of the next year. Fargo pioneer and Herbst family friend George Upham had the distinct honor of turning over the first spade of dirt. He was present at the opening of the original store in 1892.

For the building expansion project, a 38-by-100-foot section of the Edwards Building to the north was torn down so that the Herbst building could add more floor space. This photograph taken on July 14, 1924, shows the I-beams filling the space once occupied by the Edwards Building.

The expansion also added two additional stories to the building. This increased the working floor space from 25,000 to 73,000 square feet. This view shows the top two floors in the midst of construction, taken from the roof of the old building. The new building was designed by Fargo architect William F. Kurke.

This elevated view over the construction site was taken on July 14, 1924, from the top of the neighboring Luger Building, looking northwest. The Meinecke & Johnson Company of Fargo was the general contractor for the project. In this image, a few construction workers are visible laying the new roof top.

The Herbst Department Store remained open all through the expansion project in 1924. In order to entice customers, the window displays continued to be filled with merchandise, and signs painted with large arrows pointed the way toward the temporary entrance at right. This all took place while construction workers plied their trade on the surrounding ladders and scaffolding.

This view shows the ready-to-wear department in the midst of renovation in September 1924. At the time, it was located on the second floor of what was the old portion of the building, as construction and demolition took place all around it. A temporary wall stands along the right side of the room.

This photograph, taken in September 1924, features the domestics department, located in an unfinished portion of the newly constructed building. One can imagine that the employees were kept busy moving the merchandise around from location to location, while customers were in the store shopping.

With construction nearing its end, pedestrians walk past the open north entrance and store window awaiting glass installation. The new building featured 140 feet of new window space, which was comprised of three large display windows and two island-style show windows. This allowed the display of merchandise from many departments of the store at the same time.

This photograph of the building was taken shortly after completion, showing the new front façade featuring white- and cream-enameled terra-cotta, which faced the building from sidewalk to parapet. Original plans called for a 75-foot advertising signal tower to be erected on the roof that would contain a high-voltage light visible 50 to 60 miles away. This apparently never materialized.

Two Otis Micro-Drive Self-Leveling passenger elevators were installed in the new store. These elevators brought the car platform level with the floor, regardless of the skill of the operator. The self-leveling feature also eliminated abrupt reversals and trip hazards, giving the passengers a more secure ride. They ran from the basement to the fourth floor. One freight elevator was also installed in the rear of the new building.

This is the completed section of the second floor prior to occupation. The new building had 55,000 square feet of maple flooring and a total of 1.75 miles of pipe for the automatic fire-sprinkler system, some of which can be seen suspended from the ceiling.

The grand reopening of the new store took place on May 12, 1926. Here a woman enters the building with a baby carriage through one of the two entrances that were designed to provide easy entry and exit without overcrowding. Each of the entrances had three doors.

This photograph shows the crowded conditions of the old store, with merchandise spilling over into the narrow aisles. In order to see the silk goods at right, customers and employees had to move the bolts of fabric and chairs that appear to be in the way. The necessities of the expansion are obvious, especially when compared with the photograph of the new store below.

This photograph taken in 1926 shows the main floor of the new store. The new construction provided wider aisles and better display arrangements. A store directory from the time lists the following items on the main floor: silks, woolens, wash goods, domestics, linens, handkerchiefs, shoes, music notions, trimmings, patterns, hosiery, floral, toilet goods, jewelry, neckwear, leather goods, gloves, umbrellas, linings, ribbons, candy, and bargain tables.

The basement of the new building featured a bargain section. The new ventilation system changed the air in the basement every 10 minutes with clean filtered air. The bright lighting, wide aisles, and high ceilings provided a pleasant atmosphere for shoppers to find great deals on discounted merchandise. Two signs suspended from the ceiling announce, "Bargains everywhere."

This 1936 view looks south on the sidewalk in front of the Herbst Department Store. At this time, a new electric neon sign was being added to the front of the store to better attract shoppers from street level. It was believed to be the largest neon sign in the Northwest.

The new sign was dedicated on May 16, 1936, as part of the Herbst Department Store's 44th anniversary celebration. One of the store's oldest living customers, 77-year-old Elizabeth Hill, flipped the switch, which illuminated the 38-foot-high sign with huge red neon letters spelling out Herbst.

This elevated view from April 1940 looks out over the main floor of the store. The view shows a wide array of merchandise for sale. In the foreground are display cases filled with perfume, jewelry, and handbags. In the back of the room are shoes, books, fabric, and lingerie.

In July 1954, a 100-horsepower air-cooling plant was installed in the Herbst building that provided air conditioning on all four floors. The system was designed by North Central Engineers and installed by the Sornsin Company. The cooling effect was equal to melting 160,000 pounds of ice per day. This photograph of the street-level floor was taken in the early 1960s.

In October 1958, the Herbst Department Store acquired Luger Furniture Company, the business that occupied the neighboring building to the south (at left). The Luger Furniture Company had been in business since 1878. The acquisition added 32,000 square feet of space and expanded the Broadway frontage to 131 feet.

The acquisition of the Luger store allowed Herbst to greatly expand its fine home-furnishings operation, as well as relocate and enlarge several other departments. Here is a view of the furniture department, located on the second floor of the Luger building, as it appeared in March 1966.

The 1960s ushered in many changes. This started with the development of a large back parking lot west of the building. Prior to this, the store advertised a lot at Broadway and First Avenue South, a two-block walk from the store. The new lot was built in cooperation with First National Bank in 1961 and required the removal of the Nash-Finch warehouse.

The new parking lot brought more attention to the west side of the building. The little-used doorway that once opened into an alley became a well-trafficked entry into the store. This view from May 1967 features the rear entrance as well as signs celebrating the store's diamond anniversary.

This photograph of the main floor of Herbst was taken in 1966. It reveals a more modernized look with newer merchandise cases, cabinets, and florescent lighting, all to enhance the shopping experience. Former store employee Byron Bergman related the story of actress and singer Pearl Bailey losing track of time while shopping for Christmas gifts at Herbst's and missing her appointment to appear on WDAY-TV's program *Party Line*.

In 1963, the S&H Green Stamp redemption center was opened on the third floor of the Luger building. These trading stamps were distributed by participating stores around the country. A customer received stamps based upon the dollar amount of their purchases and pasted the stamps into a booklet. When the booklet was filled, customers could trade them in for premiums toward merchandise from participating stores.

In September 1966, it was announced that the Herbst Department Store was to receive a new front façade. The facelift was designed by the Fargo architecture firm Seifert and Staszko Associates, and the general contractor was John T. Jones Construction Company. In this photograph, workers have begun blocking up the windows.

The update was meant to unify the Luger Building with the Herbst building and provide a more modern look to the store. The project was projected to cost $75,000, with completion around the middle of November 1966, just in time for the store's 75th anniversary the following year.

As part of this renovation, the Luger building received a new entrance. At street level, both buildings received new granite facing with steel molding around the display windows. Here, a contractor is working on the new entrance and display windows at the Luger portion of the building. The "Luger" in front of the door was left in place.

The upper levels of the building were clad in a soft-tone porcelain on aluminum, separated by gold Aggretex columns. The new Herbst marquee was installed using black accent letters with backlighting. The new façade extended across approximately 131 feet of frontage. The sign to the left says, "Herbst is putting on a new face for you and downtown Fargo."

In June 1966, Herbst bought the neighboring Edwards Building at 22 Broadway, and in the summer of 1968, the building was extensively renovated. On the main floor, Herbst leased space to the S&L Department Store and Bob Fritz Sporting Goods. The main floor would also become the home of Herbst Travel Agency.

In the renovation of the Edwards Building, the second floor was completely remodeled to accommodate several Herbst departments, including lingerie and domestics. A section of the wall between the Herbst Building and the Edwards Building was opened up to give easy access to the new floor space. In this image, a portion of the old roof is lowered onto Northern Pacific Avenue.

The third floor of the Edwards Building was completely removed. This was done so that the second floor ceilings could be extended upward, giving the new additional store space a more open feel. These two contractors are in the process of manually demolishing the building's 65-year-old brick walls on the west side of the building.

At the same time as all the other renovations, the interior of the store also underwent updates. Several departments were reconfigured and expanded to increase customer convenience. This view is looking northwest over the main showroom floor, decorated for the Herbst Citrus Day promotion in April 1968. Orange crates are suspended from the ceiling.

In the 1970s, Herbst Department Store expanded operations to other North Dakota locations. In 1971, branch stores were opened in Devils Lake and Bismarck. In August 1972, a branch was opened in the new West Acres Shopping Center in Fargo, and in 1976, a branch was opened in Jamestown. This image of West Acres was taken in 1977.

On the evening of January 4, 1974, a fire struck the Luger wing of the Herbst Department Store. The fire started in the furnace room, located in the southwest corner of the building, and spread up a nearby elevator shaft. Firefighters were able to extinguish the fire by pumping water down the shaft and into the basement. This photograph, taken after the fire, shows the rear of the building where the fire started.

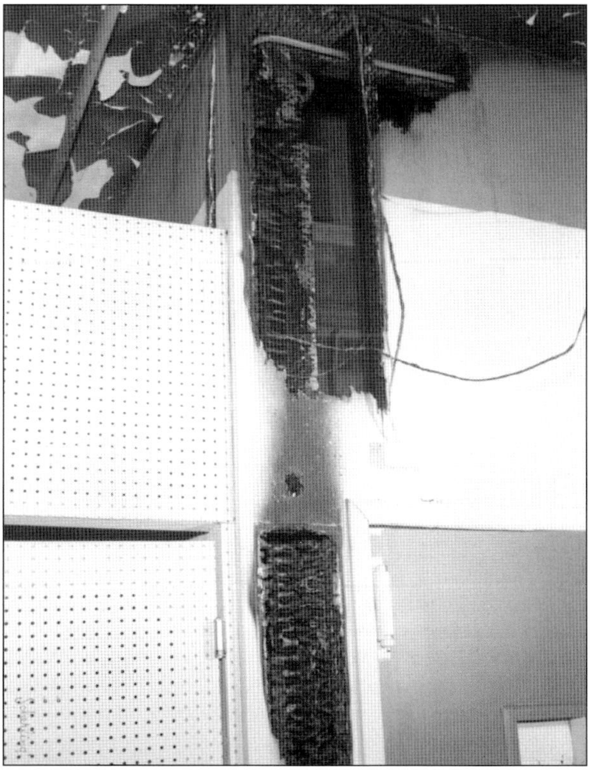

Damage was extensive in the furnace room, and a considerable amount of new merchandise was lost in the nearby shipping-receiving and marking rooms. Portions of the basement floor buckled, and much of the building suffered smoke and water damage. The store was closed for business until early February, when Herbst held a fire sale. It took a number of months for the store to recover from this disaster.

Several Herbst employees posed on earthmoving equipment during the construction of the Red River Mall in 1974. The project was designed to curtail heavy traffic on Broadway and make a more pedestrian friendly shopping experience for downtown Fargo. At the time, several retail stores had abandoned their downtown buildings for West Acres Shopping Center. This started a steady decline for downtown as a retail destination.

At the same time that the Red River Mall project was underway, the store was going through a $250,000 post-fire remodeling and redecoration. On September 16, 1974, Herbst celebrated the completion of the remodel with a book signing by actor Gregory Peck. This is the storefront as it appeared in January 1975.

Bob Herbst, who was serving as president of the chamber of commerce at the time, was optimistic that the Red River Mall would save downtown, but with time, the narrow winding street, canopy, concrete posts, and flower planters proved ineffective and were eventually removed. This photograph of Herbst and the mall was taken in January 1975.

In 1975, Richard Herbst and several partners opened up the Old Broadway restaurant and lounge on the main floor of the Edwards Building, after the S&L store went out of business. This Herbst clothing model is seated at the bar of the restaurant. This group, the Herbst Development Company, also was responsible for the Southgate Racquet Club, the Grainery restaurant, and Oxbow Country Club near Hickson, North Dakota.

By the late 1970s, an economic downturn and the vanishing downtown retail climate was disastrous for Herbst. In 1979, the West Acres and Devils Lake branch stores were sold to Braun's, a firm out of Minneapolis. The main store had become dependent on promotional sales to bring shoppers downtown. This brought in large crowds but was unsustainable and did not make enough money.

In October 1981, it was announced that Herbst, the last department store in downtown Fargo, was going out of business. In December 1981, the Jamestown store was closed, and on February 15, 1982, the main store closed after 90 years of business. The three buildings that made up Herbst were remodeled into a business complex called Broadway Park, with the front façades of the buildings restored to their original appearance.

Three

THE STORE'S DEPARTMENTS

During the store's first decade of business, it featured silks, linens, parasols, hosiery, gloves, laces, washable fabrics, and notions. The millinery department held the latest imported and domestic designs. There were clothes and footwear available for men, women, and children. The store also had a large line of house furnishing, curtains, hardware, tinware, and novelties. The large variety of stock available at Herbst can be seen in this pre-1925 photograph.

In 1933, a large section of the second floor was named the Fashion Floor, and this name was used in advertisements for the next three decades. It featured clothing for boys, infants, and juniors. For women, it had coats, suits, dresses, sportswear, cottonwear, corsets, foundations, furs, and hats. This view shows the women's departments on the Fashion Floor as it appeared in July 1937.

This general view of the Fashion Floor from April 1940 shows women's hats, dresses, and blouses on display in a warm and welcoming space. The floor contained dozens of mirrors and dressing rooms as well as experienced clerks. There was also an alterations department with expert fitters and modern equipment.

This view of the Economee Fashions section from the 1930s features ready-to-wear dresses arranged on the racks by their sizes. Ready-to-wear was factory-made clothing designed and made in standardized sizes that fit the frames of most women. This was opposed to clothing made to measure by a tailor. This mass-produced clothing was usually a less expensive option to customers.

This 1936 display was set up in the women's sportswear section, which was located on the Fashion Floor. It featured clothing for women with an active lifestyle. This included athletic wear, slacks, skirts, blouses, sweaters, hats, and daytime frocks.

The women's sportswear section also carried swimwear. Here is a view of the beach shop from July 1937, which prominently features swimwear from Jantzen. With Fargo's proximity to Minnesota's many lakes, Herbst could cater to those women who had the ability and desire to enjoy water recreation.

A millinery, or hat department, can be found listed in some of the earliest Herbst store descriptions and advertisements. This view of the department from July 1937 shows a variety of hats displayed on mannequin heads. An advertisement from the time listed the availability of bandeaus, bretons, gobs, profile and big brims, and turban hat types. This department also sold a wide variety of wigs.

The Fashion Floor was also the home to the corset department. Pictured here is a Modart-brand corset display from 1926. This department featured private fitting rooms where expert corsetieres could measure the customers to make sure the corsets and brassieres fit properly.

According to a 1926 newspaper article about the Herbst corset shop, the corsetiere was trained to believe that the value in correct corseting was the foundation for all outward appearance. In fact, the department was often referred to as the foundations department. This view of the department was taken in July 1937.

This photograph of the baby shop was taken in the late 1920s. At the time, it was located on the second floor of the building. The shop sold all things related to infants, including clothing, furniture, and dainty novelties for a baby's amusement. There was a separate layette room adjoining the main infant department that dealt specifically with all things for newborns.

This view of the baby shop from the early 1940s shows the clerks dressed in white, simulating nurse uniforms. The store took a great interest in the health and wellbeing of their smallest customers. The store offered a baby clinic in which parents could bring their infants in to receive a medical exam. The names of the babies were entered into a drawing, and the winners would receive monogrammed cups and merchandise certificates.

This view of the Junior Shop, featuring clothing for young girls, was taken in the late 1930s. At the time, the shop was located on the Fashion Floor of the building. Prominently displayed is a cardboard cutout of Shirley Temple, who was all the rage at the time. One 1937 Herbst style show featured five Fargo girls who were contenders in a national Shirley Temple look-alike contest.

The hosiery department was always located on the street level of the store. This view shows how the department appeared in 1926, shortly after the building expansion. At the time, they were selling stockings for not only women but men and children as well. This included the brands Bobolinks, Phoenix, Strutwear, Munsingwear, Iron Clad, Cadet, Onyx, Van Raalte, and Eiffel.

Here is a view of the hosiery department as it appeared on April 12, 1940. At the time, it was located on the street level, in the southeast corner near the front entrance. Herbst had gained a reputation for quality products at reasonable prices. Customer service was important; if the stockings did not wear well or were defective, they could be returned, and the store would make it right.

The store also had a long history of selling fabric by the yard. It was not uncommon for people to make their own clothing, and the store carried a large variety of silks, woolens, cottons, and washable goods. They also carried Butterick and McCall sewing patterns and offered sewing classes. The fabric department is pictured here in April 1940, in the rear of the store at street level.

In 1937, a mother traveling on the Great Northern Empire Builder became concerned that her child's feet were getting cold. So, she had the conductor wire ahead to Fargo, with a request that some children's footwear be brought to the depot. Herbst was contacted, and an assortment of shoes were sent over. The mother did her shopping and satisfied her need. This photograph of the shoe department was taken in 1926.

This view of the women's shoe department is from 1966. This department space was leased to a shoe distributor and was always located at street level toward the back of the building. Some of the shoe brands available at Herbst were Larks, Corelli, Connie, Capri, Naturalizer, Giardino, and Jacqueline.

From the earliest years of business, this Herbst department was called toiletries, but by the mid-1950s it was named cosmetics. The department was located on street level and featured a variety of items, including soaps, perfumes, colognes, and makeup. This busy day at the cosmetics counter was during the Salute to Italy event in September 1971.

The men's department was always located on the street level of the Herbst building, usually near the front doors. This photograph was taken in March 1966. Visible are display cases with an assortment of packaged men's dress shirts.

The Lion's Den was opened in 1966 on the lower level of the south building, a space that once belonged to Luger Furniture, until its merger with Herbst in 1959. This department was developed to cater to young men. The space was decorated in dark oak woods and masculine décor, and was staffed by sales personnel who were trained in fashions that appealed to this demographic.

These two shoppers are checking out the selection of suitcases found in the luggage department in 1966. At the time, Herbst was carrying a wide selection of suitcases, shoulder totes, and duffle bags made by Samsonite. Posters along the wall advertise the many places a customer could visit.

The Herbst family had a great interest in travel, and this was reflected in their decision to open Herbst International Travel in September 1967. It was first located on the lower level of the building and later moved to the Edwards Building. As part of the 1971 Salute to Italy event, the store brought in Pan Am flight attendant Marilyn Allen to give a demonstration on how to pack a suitcase.

This Russell Stover candy display from 1966 was on the street level, conveniently located next to the greeting cards, stationery, fresh-cut flowers, and gift-wrapping paper. The location made it easy for quick, in-and-out shopping if need be. Herbst also had a more extensive gift area on the lower level of the building.

The china and glassware department, pictured here in the late 1960s, was always located on the lower level of the Herbst Building. At this time, the store was selling Oxford Bone, Royal Doulton, Lenox, and Syracuse china. China was a popular wedding gift, and engaged couples could set up a wedding-gift registry that included their chosen make and pattern.

This Herbst saleswoman is showing a customer a Brownie Starmite II camera by Kodak, which was produced between 1962 and 1967. This was one of the many products being sold by the camera department, located on the street level in the south building. They also carried movie cameras, projectors, film, flashbulbs, projection screens, photo albums, and other camera-related merchandise. The department was operated by Epko Film Service.

Herbst also leased space on the street level of the south building to Walden Book Company. Besides books, this department also carried posters and art-reproduction prints. In this image, Connie Atkinson (center) and two other employees are looking through some of the titles available in the children's section in the early 1970s.

This overview of the record department was taken around Christmas 1962. From at least 1926, the store had a music department. For most of the time, this department was located at street level. The department sold everything from top-40 singles to Lawrence Welk. If one wished to listen to a record before purchase, a clerk could play it.

This broad view of the television and stereo center, located on the second floor of the south building, was taken in March 1966. The *Herbstime* radio program, featuring Manny Marget, was broadcast live over KVOX Radio from this department during the 1960s.

These four salesmen from the television and stereo department are gathered around an RCA Victor Console color television called the Staunton. It was the featured television in the 75th-anniversary sale in March 1967. The advertisement describes it as "Early American Styling in beautiful Antiqued Colonial maple." The sale price was $417.

Advertisements from the 1930s show Herbst selling gas stoves and washing machines as part of their furniture department on the third floor. As the appliance selection increased, it was moved to the lower level, and then to the second floor of the Luger building in 1959. Eventually, the department, pictured here in 1966, was leased by Homemakers Villa.

These bargain shoppers are checking out discounted merchandise in the housewares department during the fire sale of 1974. Being on the lower level of the building, this department would have suffered some of the worst smoke and water damage after the fire on January 4. The sign hanging from the ceiling reassures customers that all damaged merchandise had been removed and was not for sale.

These two salespeople stand among a line of Hoover vacuum cleaners. The two vacuums featured front and center are the Hoover model 575, which was produced in 1929. Often, Herbst would advertise vacuum cleaners with rug sales, as it was a logical sales combination. The store offered expert Hoover vacuum repair and service.

On September 7, 1928, the store opened its furniture department on the third floor of the building. The department included the latest makes and designs in home furnishing, including this Art Deco bedroom set by New York designer Gilbert Rohde in 1935. By featuring this modern style of furniture, Herbst was bringing sophistication and style to Fargo and the region.

When the furniture department opened, it included an interior-design section and a drapery department. This overview from the late 1930s shows the drapery department and the needle-art department in the background. Although located on the third floor, a freight elevator simplified movement of the pieces. In 1959, the expanded furniture department moved to the second floor of the south building.

This view of the bargain basement is from 1924, during the building expansion. The store was trying to reduce its merchandise by having "A Whale of a Sale." This photograph features a large selection of merchandise ranging from domestics, wash goods, and fabric remnants to shoes.

The Herbst Beauty Salon was located on the third floor of the Herbst building after the 1926 expansion. An advertisement from the time states that it had trained experts "specializing on hair bobbing, marcelling, permanent waving by the Paul Oil Method, manicuring and scalp treatments."

In 1957, the salon went through a major renovation. This included seven open-styling workstations and new equipment throughout, including automatic heat-regulated hair dryers. The décor was rose and blue with wide mirrors. This view shows the waiting area of the salon as it appeared in March 1966. By the 1970s, the salon was leased by Glemby International, a beauty-salon company.

A space first known as the tea room was part of the building expansion in 1926. It was located in the balcony overlooking the street level of the store. The tea room provided a space where shoppers could rest and enjoy lunch, a cup of coffee, or even a soda from the soda fountain.

Around 1933, the Herbst cafeteria opened on the lower level of the building, where it remained until the store closed. It was a popular spot for downtown customers and businesspeople to take in a meal. Reservations could be made for luncheons and meetings, and catering could be arranged for community events and parties. This photograph captures a busy lunch hour in 1966.

The cafeteria underwent a complete remodeling in 1956. Everything was replaced, including the tables, air-conditioning, lighting, and floor tiles. Additionally, a new bakery was added to the kitchen area in the back. Anna Raaum (left) and an unidentified waitress are stocking the dessert case in this 1967 photograph.

In this photograph from 1967, an unidentified Herbst cook and Tina Mattson (right) are making mashed potatoes and baked chicken in the kitchen. In 1974, the cafeteria was renovated as a result of smoke and water damage from a fire that took place in January. At that time, the dining room was expanded to seat 125 people.

Herbst offered a mail-order service. Orders that were received by mail were filled and mailed out the same day. A 1926 advertisement stated, "Whether it be a toothpick or a piano," every mail order would receive as prompt attention as though the customer was at the store in person. This 1936 delivery truck would make deliveries in Fargo and Moorhead each day.

In a 1937 advertisement, Herbst offered free delivery up to 200 miles on purchases of $20 or more. The Herbst delivery service was still going strong in 1967, when this photograph was taken. At this time, the store was selling large merchandise such as rugs, carpet, appliances, and furniture.

Four

HERBST EMPLOYEES

These two clerks were ready and eager to help out customers in the fabric department. Axel Larsen (left) worked at Herbst from about 1899 to 1911. Mark Holderman (right), the "silk man," worked at Herbst from around 1896 to 1907. Holderman was a Civil War veteran who served with the Ohio Infantry.

Pictured here in 1910 are, from left to right, Stanley Marcks, window trimmer; Frederick Collier, from the wool goods department; and Otto Johnson, from the silk department, standing proudly in front of their window display. Ike Herbst was one of the first store owners in Fargo to display his merchandise in the store windows.

Herbst Department Store employees stand in front of the store and peer out of the windows on June 19, 1910, two days before founder Ike Herbst's unexpected death. A row of cars are parked behind them. The store appears to be decorated for an event, as American flags and stars adorn the windows.

Emma Herbst was key in creating a close-knit group of employees. At the 1920 store Christmas party, she suggested that an employees' club be organized, and donated $500 to the cause. A week later, the Herbst Social and Benefit Club, known as the S&B Club, was founded. The club sponsored social events like this dinner in the early 1920s.

The Yama Yamma Chorus entertains at an S&B Club event in 1922. Each employee paid one percent of his or her salary to the club, and the store matched each dollar. By being a part of the club, employees received sick benefits, death benefits, flowers and visitors when ill, and entertainment events. The club lasted until the store closed in 1982.

The Herbst Department Store orchestra poses for a group photograph on March 14, 1923. The members were, in no particular order, Dee Dee Addington, Chuck Man, A. Johnson, Thayne Boughton, Don Cowan, Reuben Zalk, George Carter, and Stan Cowan. They played for the spring fashion show that day. The event also featured a whistling soloist.

On May 23, 1922, Herbst employees and family members gathered for a group outing. The young men in front carry instruments, including a large drum emblazoned with "Fargo Boy Scout" on the front. "The Reds Eat on the Blues" may refer to sales competitions that employees had to win prizes. Teams of employees would be assigned different colors.

The S&B Club is gathered for a Christmas party in 1922 at the Commercial Club. A Christmas tree stands in the back to the right of the support pillar, and Krohn Herbst sits in the front row in the middle. The older woman standing directly to the left of the pillar is most likely Emma Herbst.

These 10 employees, the Herbst Beauty Chorus, probably worked in the beauty salon. The ladies wearing matching coveralls have combs in their pockets and sport stylish 1920s–1930s haircuts. An advertisement from 1933 indicates that for $1, a woman could get a Tarola treatment shampoo and finger wave, a facial arch, or a shampoo, finger wave, and manicure.

These young women show some of the popular hairstyles of the 1920s and 1930s. The finger wave and Marcel, worn by many of these women, looked similar, but were created by different methods. The finger wave was created by placing the hair between fingers and combing the hair in alternating directions. The Marcel was created with a curling iron. Both methods were available at the Herbst beauty salon.

It was tradition for the Herbst Department Store staff to pose for a group portrait in costumes for the store anniversary. The 44th anniversary, in 1936, had a farmyard theme. Staff dressed in farmer outfits, and two employees dressed up as a cow. A little boy in the center of the photograph holds an old-fashioned Mickey Mouse doll.

On February 29, 1940, gender roles were switched, and the women employees were put in charge of the Herbst Department Store for a day. Seated from left to right are Margaret Wyatt (acting advertising manager), Doris Nelson (personal shopper), Hilda Forsyth (third-floor manager), Sylvia Rutz (president), Idah Gustafson (personnel manager), Joyce Phillips (display manager), and Peggy Johnson (promotion manager). Standing from left to right are Eva May King (merchandise manager), Virgil Jones (general manager), and Ann Rood (secretary-treasurer).

For the Herbst Department Store's 58th anniversary sale in 1950, the staff dressed as Native Americans. By this year, the department store had about 250 employees. They may be preparing for the Fargo Diamond Jubilee parade that occurred on June 5, 1950. Robert K. Herbst served on the jubilee advisory committee. Fargo was incorporated on January 5, 1875.

The 59th anniversary of the Herbst Department Store, in 1951, had a circus theme. Store staff went all out dressing up as clowns, trapeze artists, and in other silly outfits, including Mickey Mouse. Once again, an employee dressed up as an animal, this time a baby elephant.

The Herbst Department Store's 60th Anniversary, celebrated on May 9, 1952, also had a circus theme. The employees are, from left to right, Nevada Savageau (jewelry department), Carrie Ashelman (marking room), Martena Clements (alterations department), and Clara Pladson (alterations department).

Pictured from left to right are Gloria Tronson from the beauty salon, salesman Harold Bredemeier, and Judy Volk from the needle-art department. They mug for the camera at the Herbst Department Store's 60th anniversary employee dinner on May 9, 1952. They are dressed up for the circus theme.

The circus theme for the 60th anniversary celebration was not complete without two "Freak Zombies from the Outer Darkness." These two lovely zombies are Violet Clearwater (left) from the lingerie department and Amanda "Honey" Egge, the manager and buyer of the lingerie and cosmetics department, who worked at Herbst for 17 years.

Michael Herbst shakes employee Louise Sale's hand and proffers a gift while Richard Herbst looks on at the 75th anniversary celebration in the Elks Club ballroom in 1967. Sale was employed as a seamstress and worked her way up to manager of the alterations department. She worked for the store for about 30 years.

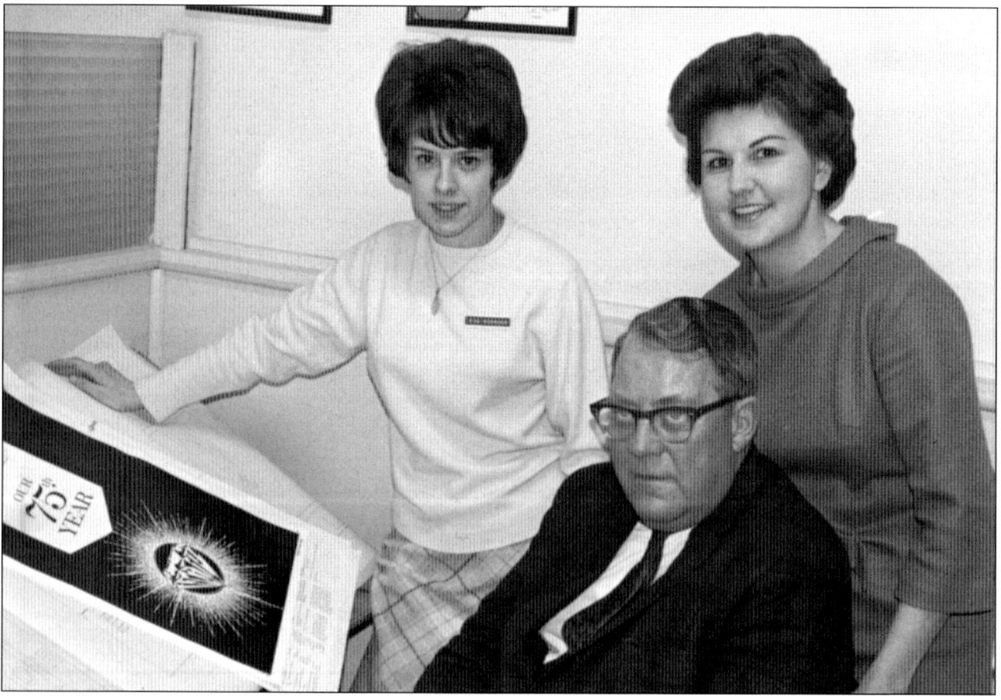

In 1967, the Herbst Department Store celebrated its diamond jubilee. Advertising manager Russell Lane, Mary Georgeson (left) and another employee admire an advertisement created for the 75th anniversary of the store, which ran in the *Forum* newspaper on March 5. A sale was held the next day. Throughout the rest of the year, monthly drawings were held for diamond rings and US savings bonds.

Two Herbst Department Store employees pose with records in the books and music department. Connie Atkinson (left) holds a copy of *Esquire's World of Humor*, edited by Lewis W. Gillenson. The younger woman holds an album by Herb Alpert & the Tijuana Brass, a Latin music group. This album sold for $3.98. Herbst leased space to Walden Books instead of running the book department itself.

A Herbst Department Store employee works diligently at a graphotype machine. This machine embossed small plates of sheet metal, typically dog tags. This machine was probably used to emboss address tags, which were then inked and stamped onto envelopes. Thus, this employee probably worked in the mail room.

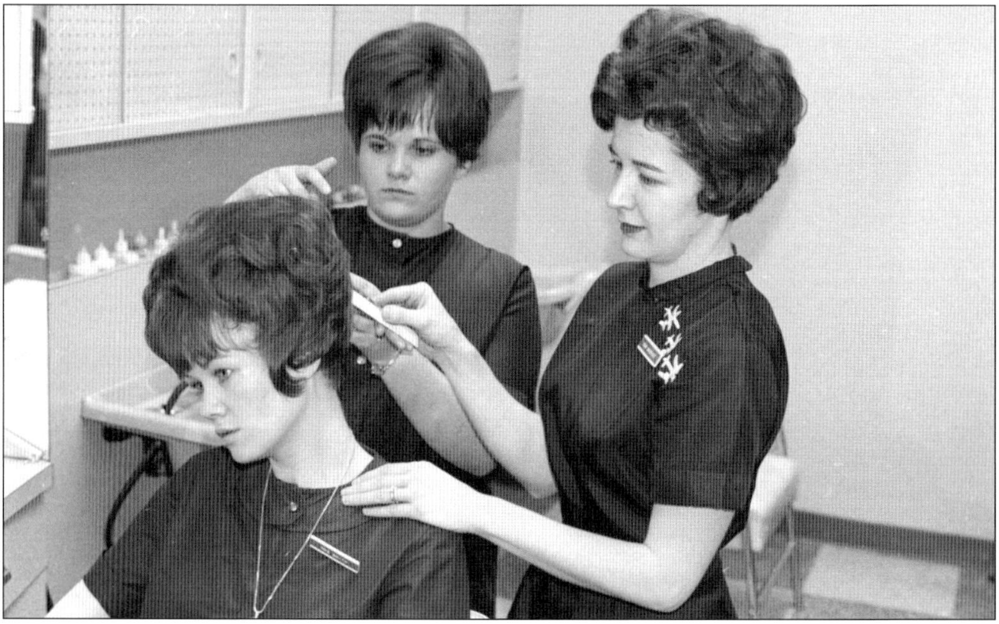

Employees of the Herbst Department Store's beauty salon try out some new styling techniques in 1967. Hair was backcombed in sections to give more volume. Extreme backcombing resulted in the popular beehive look, but these women settled on a more subtle, yet still voluminous, style. The woman standing at right is Agnes Schmidt, salon operator.

Saleslady Emma Thimgan arranges a display of gloves in January 1967. Ladies' gloves went on sale for $1.75 a pair for the diamond jubilee sale that started on March 6. Thimgan was born into a German Russian family from Denhoff, North Dakota. She worked many years in retail, first at Royal Jewelers, and then at Herbst, until the store closed in 1982.

The Herbst Department Store had its own telephone switchboard and operator. This switchboard, known as a private-branch exchange, allowed the switchboard operator to rout incoming calls to any of the various telephones throughout the store. Alyce Lechner started working as a switchboard operator in 1958, then later moved to the credit department.

In 1966, Joseph I. Connors became the manager of the Lion's Den, a new clothing department for young men. Connors was originally from Galesburg, Illinois, and worked at the Palace Clothing store in Moorhead, Minnesota, before coming to the Herbst Department Store.

Byron Bergman was the Herbst Department Store's visual merchandiser from 1956 to 1980. He was responsible for all of the window displays and interior and exterior decorations for the downtown and branch locations. Instead of ordering mannequins, props, and decorations from trade shows and catalogs, Bergman and his assistants made most things by hand, purchasing supplies locally from other Fargo stores.

Audrey McConnell (right) was department manager and worked at Herbst from the late 1950s until the store closed in 1982. She shows off a stylish shirt with another employee. The Herbst employees maintained a strong bond with each other, even after the store closed. Many of them formed a group called the Old Shoes, and they would meet to reminisce about the old days.

Five

STORE EVENTS

On Thanksgiving Day 1922, a barnstorming stunt was supposed to bring Santa Claus to the Herbst Department Store, touted as the "First Aerial Delivery in North Dakota." That morning, a winter storm prevented the airplane from making the trip, burying it in snow up to the wings. November blizzards are not uncommon in Fargo.

This 1930s Santa flight appears to have been more successful than the 1922 flight. Krohn Herbst was very interested in aviation, and backed Moorhead aviatrix Florence Klingensmith. He was one of the businessmen in town who assisted her with the purchase of her first plane. When she was killed in a 1933 crash, he was one of the pallbearers at her funeral.

A crowd anxiously awaits for the doors to open for Herbst's first Dollar Day Sale, on May 23, 1923. This popular sale was held every 90 days. It featured a large number of unique items for $1. Six times a day a gong would ring, and one high-value item would be placed somewhere within the store. The first customer who found it could buy it for $1.

North Dakota's oldest binder was displayed on the Herbst showroom floor as part of this farmers' festival in the late 1920s. Likely such a display would have attracted business from the many rural agricultural laborers drawn to the Red River Valley for the annual fall harvest. Supposedly, this binder was still in working order.

During the Fire Prevention Week of 1928, Herbst Department Store was used by the fire department to demonstrate fire-saving techniques. The week surrounding October 9, the anniversary of the Great Chicago Fire, was proclaimed Fire Prevention Week by Pres. Woodrow Wilson in 1920.

Probably one of the more interesting events at Herbst took place with the visit of Edna Kirby, the Paramount Girl. This promotional stunt featured Kirby (third from right), a relatively low-grade motion-picture actress from Hollywood, living in the display windows of the store for a week. Here she poses with Krohn Herbst (fourth from left) and other dignitaries at Hector Airport on September 10, 1928.

Edna Kirby was greeted by Fargo mayor J.H. Dahl upon her arrival, and then took up residence in her "Apartment Unique." Living a week behind glass, she used and demonstrated merchandise that could be purchased in the store. A daily schedule was published in the *Forum* newspaper so that the public would know what they could see at any given point in the day.

This photograph taken in December 1930 shows a children's sewing class. The Herbst Department Store often supplied space for community-education programs. Often, these classes were taught by extension agents and instructors from the nearby North Dakota Agricultural College. Such classes taught young girls how to create outfits using fabric that could be purchased from the store, and ultimately created lifelong customers.

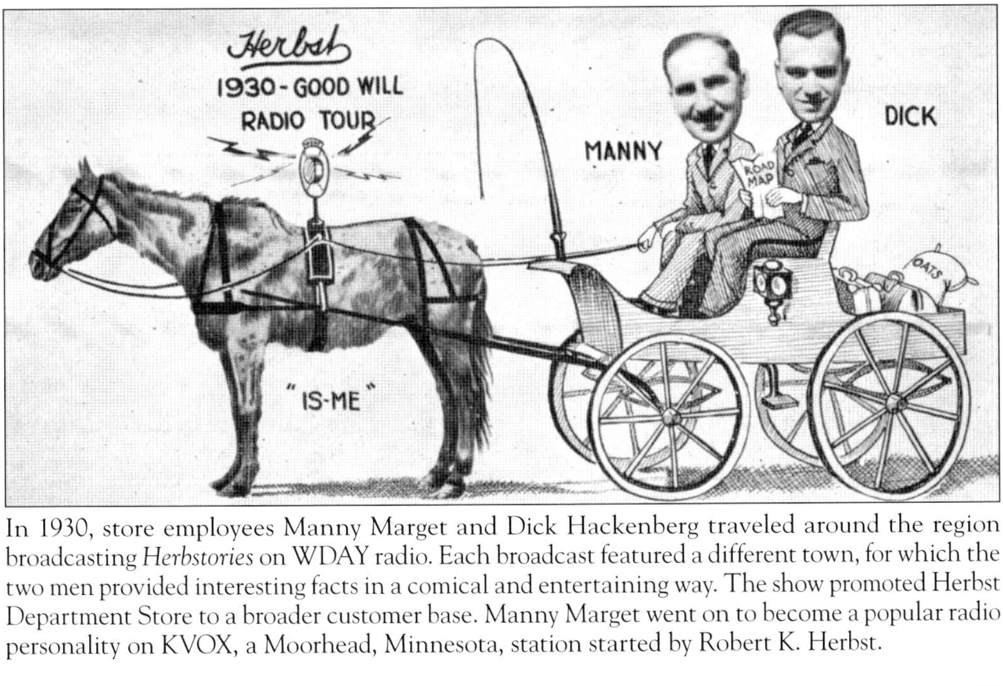

In 1930, store employees Manny Marget and Dick Hackenberg traveled around the region broadcasting *Herbstories* on WDAY radio. Each broadcast featured a different town, for which the two men provided interesting facts in a comical and entertaining way. The show promoted Herbst Department Store to a broader customer base. Manny Marget went on to become a popular radio personality on KVOX, a Moorhead, Minnesota, station started by Robert K. Herbst.

A fire-truck ladder is being used to decorate Broadway in front of Herbst in December 1931. The building is festooned with real evergreen trees, an inexpensive way of decorating at the height of the Great Depression. In 1932, Krohn Herbst, then chair of the chamber of commerce, announced Fargo's decoration project, which would put investment into sturdier trimmings that would last an extended time.

The Blossom Time hosiery party was held at Herbst in April 1930. The party was not a sale, but rather a promotional event to educate women on the proper care of silk hosiery. The department was decorated as a Chinese pergola over a garden, complete with songbirds and incense burners. Salesgirls dressed in silk pajamas served tea. Most of the attendees left the party with more than one pair of hose.

These three saleswomen donned Martha Washington costumes to promote the Washington Maid silk stockings just before Mother's Day in 1934. They were likely well versed in the brand, which sold different stockings for work, play, and dress up. According to newspaper advertisements, Herbst was the only store in Fargo to carry the brand.

This photograph shows the Herbst parade float in the Jack Frost Winter Carnival, held on February 14, 1941. This carnival was an annual weeklong event, which took place during the 1940s and 1950s. The festivities usually included a parade, the crowning of the Jack Frost Queen, a dance, an ice-skating show, and ice sculptures.

With the outbreak of World War II, the Office of Civil Defense prepared and educated the civilian population for the possibility of air raids on American soil. This first-aid class was taught to Herbst employees by the Red Cross in July 1942 by Ralph Yoder, who ran the ambulance service in Fargo at the time.

July 17, 1942, was National Heroes Day, and Fargo retailers erected sidewalk booths on every block of the business district to sell war bonds and stamps. This was the Herbst booth for this event. From left to right are William P. Chestnut from the chamber of commerce, and store employees Ellen Endersbe, Alice Nordstrom, Lorraine Lee, and Christie Stevens.

Herbst opened the Victory Bond Window for the second US war bond drive on April 13, 1943. People could walk into the space and purchase their bonds, and receive them immediately. The patron could also sign a scroll bound for the soldiers in the 164th infantry.

Americans were asked to sacrifice for the war effort. Various drives were set up by the government to collect materials, including used books, waste fats, tin cans, scrap metal, and silk and nylon hose. Here, a large pile of scrap metal is piled up on Broadway in front of the Herbst building.

A South Pacific theme was part of this promotional party for one of the war bond drives. Herbst Department Store was fully engaged in supporting the war effort. During World War II, the US government conducted eight drives, raising $185.7 billion from 85 million Americans.

During the war, nylon production went toward parachutes, cords, and ropes. Once the war ended, it took a while for manufacturers to bring production of rationed materials back to normal. Companies making nylon hosiery could not meet the demand. This caused nylon riots to break out across the country as small shipments arrived at stores. One such sale, without a riot, took place at Herbst on February 2, 1946.

The news of the hosiery shipment was not advertised by Herbst, but word spread, and soon people were crammed into the lobby waiting to enter the store. The crowd lined up around the block in minus-18-degree weather to get their hands on this small shipment. Eventually, production was able to meet demand.

This young girl, the daughter of a Herbst employee, receives a gift from Santa Claus at this S&B Club–sponsored Christmas Party on December 12, 1948, at the Fargo Elk's Club. The employee-run club provided entertainment, decorations, and gifts for the event.

In May 1950, Herbst celebrated its 58th anniversary at the same time as Fargo's diamond jubilee. The citywide events included a kangaroo court complete with a jail cell and police dressed in period uniforms. The two employees locked up in this photograph were merchandise manager Juanita Phillips and supervisor Reidar Leveroos.

The sidewalk sale was an annual summer event in which downtown Fargo businesses sold merchandise from tables set up on the sidewalks in front of their stores. This customer is examining bath soaps at this 1960 sale. This same year, the chamber of commerce set up a Ferris wheel and a carousel on Broadway in front of the Herbst store. (Courtesy of Byron Bergman.)

This family is intently searching for the best bargains at the Herbst Department Store's Mammoth Midnight Sale, held September 5, 1962. This one-time sales event featured special prices from 8:00 p.m. to midnight. The sale also promoted double S&H Green Stamps, free coffee, and free parking in the new back parking lot.

The Herbst Santa Express was a special nine-car train that carried several thousand children and their parents from the Northern Pacific Railroad depot in Fargo to the depot in Casselton, North Dakota, on November 30, 1963. The train picked up Santa in Casselton and brought him back to Fargo.

Here Santa Claus is boarding the train while it was stopped in Casselton. He was accompanied by several other characters, including Yogi Bear, spacemen, clowns, and fairies. While on the train, every child received a lollipop and balloon from Santa. This event was scheduled a week earlier, but it had to be rescheduled due to the assassination of President Kennedy.

The Santa Breakfast at Herbst was held in the store cafeteria on December 6, 1967. It served about 120 underprivileged children from the Fargo and Moorhead area. Children were brought in from the Children's Village, Opportunity School, and Children's Harbor. Besides breakfast, each child received a bag of candy and a special button from Santa Claus. The children in this photograph are the three daughters of Michael Herbst.

In March 1965, the Herbst Teen Program was launched. This program won *Seventeen* magazine's AMY award (Award for Merchandizing to Youth) in 1966. This award honored department stores for original, progressive retailing, merchandising, and service efforts directed toward teenage girls. An example of this was an event called "Make a Pretty Face," where teen girls were trained in proper makeup-application techniques.

Another way that Herbst was progressive in its youth program was by starting a teenage fashion board. This 10-member group worked in the junior shop, called the Place. They picked garments and accessories that appealed to teenage girls. The board members are pictured here posing at the rear entrance of the store.

On August 8, 1967, the Herbst Department Store held a *Seventeen* magazine teen fashion show at the Fargo Memorial Auditorium. The event attracted a large crowd, and a drawing was held, giving away free clothing to the lucky winners. This group of teenage girls dressed in 1960s fashions arrive at the auditorium under a sign advertising the event.

Charlotte Lipson, merchandising coordinator for *Seventeen* magazine, was flown into Fargo to moderate the fashion show. The event featured a live rock 'n' roll band called the Uglies, and the models were the Herbst teen and college board members. Here the models take a walk on the Fargo Memorial Auditorium stage.

The Herbst teenage program provided entertainment opportunities for the youth of the community. An event called Teennight was held as part of a back-to-school promotion in 1969. Bands were brought in for entertainment, and teen board members dressed in the latest fashions available for purchase at Herbst. This boy is displaying his catch from an apple-bobbing competition, one of the many fun games that were part of the event.

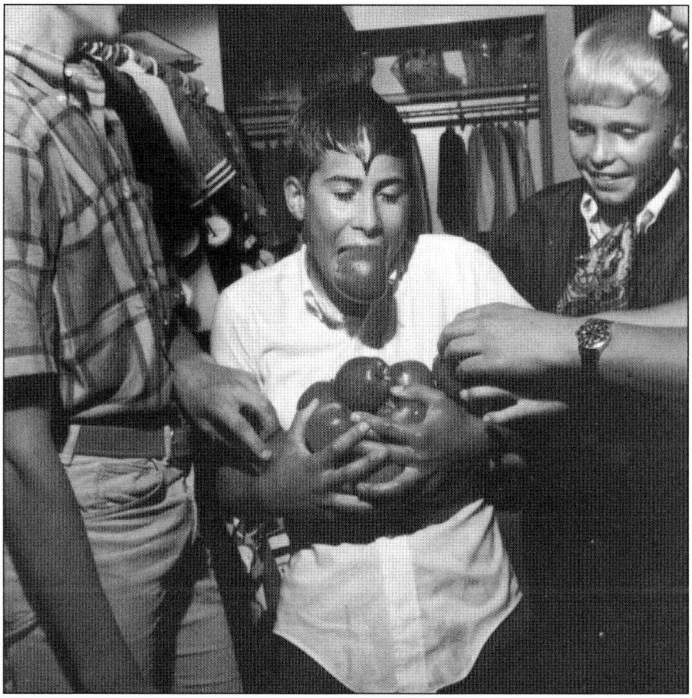

Even before the Herbst youth program was organized, dances were sponsored by the store. This dance in 1961 took place in the KVLY studios and was broadcast over the radio. Between songs, descriptions of clothing for sale at Herbst were read on the air. This event is reminiscent of the popular television show *American Bandstand* with Dick Clark.

In 1965, Herbst Department Store teamed up with KQWB radio to sponsor a rock 'n' roll band competition featuring local groups. Advertisements for the event touted it as a free back-to-school gift, since it was held during the first week of school.

Here the band Canoise from Saint Cloud, Minnesota, winners of the 1966 competition, receive their award from Fargo mayor Herschel Lashkowitz. This band was organized in the fall of 1965 and was still performing as of 2012. The band members are, from left to right, Pat Curto, Doug Swanson, Neal Dunning, and Bob Coates.

The 1967 Battle of the Bands pitted 22 groups against each other. The winner that year was the New Group from Aberdeen, South Dakota. Here, band members are signing autographs for two excited teenagers. This rhythm and blues band was inducted into the South Dakota Rock and Roll Music Association in 2015.

This view is looking out over the crowd of teenagers gathered on the Herbst Department Store's west parking lot during the 1967 Battle of the Bands. This event provided Fargo teenagers with an evening activity other than dragging Broadway. It was during this time that Fargo's elders were complaining about the evening traffic problems caused by teenagers driving their cars up and down Broadway.

Here a group of teenagers are dancing to the groovy music being performed at the Battle of the Bands. Some of the many local rock bands that performed in these competitions were the Mods, the Frantiks, and Napoleon and His Relatives. This annual competition took place over several years. One year it was held at the YMCA gymnasium and another year inside the store.

Herbst Department Store celebrated its diamond jubilee in 1967. The front façade of the building had just been refaced and was decorated to commemorate the anniversary. An exhibit showing 75 years of fashion, furniture, and antiques was set up in the basement of the store and called Gallery 75.

The diamond jubilee kicked off on March 7, 1967, with a big sale. The staff dressed in period costumes for the weeklong event. This group photograph shows the staff in their costumes. Bob Herbst is second from right in the second row, wearing the newsboy hat.

Betty Lundberg poses in her diamond jubilee costume. The costumes were the personal collection of Margaret Scott, who was the daughter of Dr. Nels Tronnes, one of the founders of Saint Luke's Hospital in Fargo. Most of the outfits had belonged to Scott's family members, and she loaned them out for special occasions.

An open house for the Herbst 75th anniversary celebrations featured treats and refreshments for guests. Frances Herbst, wife of Robert K. Herbst, is seated at right serving coffee. As part of the celebration, two television stations featured commemorative programs. The KXJB program was entitled *Salute to Progress*, and WDAY television featured *Herbst 67*. Both aired in early September 1967.

The anniversary was celebrated throughout 1967. This horse-drawn diamond jubilee Herbst wagon gave rides to visitors at the Red River Valley Fair in West Fargo. The Herbst brothers were very active supporters of the fair and Bonanzaville, USA. After the store closed, a number of artifacts from the store were donated to the museum.

The Citrus Yellow promotion took place the week of April 1–6, 1968. An advertisement for this special sales event stated, "Wherever you turn, whatever floor you are on, you'll see gay, exciting, beautiful Citrus Yellow." Models wearing this new fashion color walked the sales floors, there were citrus-cooking demonstrations, grocery stores gave away cases of citrus fruit, and a refreshment stand was set up to serve citrus drinks.

The week of October 6–12, 1968, was the Hong Kong Store Festival, sponsored by the Hong Kong Trade Development Council. A team from the organization was flown to the United States to take part in a series of department-store promotion programs. Here Rebecca Hsu, a Chinese-cooking expert, conducts a cooking demonstration for Herbst patrons.

Woon-yee Hui, an embroidery expert, demonstrated Chinese embroidery and beading work. Also at the Hong Kong Store Festival was a calligrapher who demonstrated Chinese calligraphy by writing visitors' names in Chinese characters on paper for them to take home.

The Hong Kong promotional team also brought with them a number of props for decorating the store. Here the showroom floor is decorated for the festival, complete with signs bearing Chinese calligraphy, baskets, Chinese lanterns, decorative pagodas, a dragon-dance costume, and even a fishing junk.

Salute to Italy was a two-week celebration, September 27 to October 9, 1971, in cooperation with Herbst Department Store and the Italian Ministry of Foreign Trade and Italian Government Travel Office. Here Giuseppe Avitabile, consul general of Italy, cuts a ribbon opening the event. Bob Herbst (far left) and other dignitaries look on.

Giuseppe Avitabile (second from left) and Moorhead mayor Ray Stordahl visit the Italian government travel booth set up in the Herbst Department Store on opening day of the Salute to Italy celebration. The two men standing at right are Dr. Francesco Quadrio (second from right), Italian trade commissioner, and Dr. Enrico Maggi, Italian travel commissioner.

As part of the Salute to Italy celebration, displays were set up featuring artisans from Italy and their handicrafts. This photograph shows Fulvio Cristo, a cameo-carving artist, demonstrating his skill carving miniature heads in stone, coral, and shells. Other artisans flown in for the event were a glassblower, ceramicist, and wood sculptor. At the end of the event, all their completed works were offered for sale at Herbst.

Fashion shows and photo shoots were ways that the Herbst Department Store could showcase its clothing lines. The Herbst buyers were constantly in touch with the Eastern markets, making selections of the latest styles. This female model from the 1910s poses for a photograph showing one of the ready-to-wear fashions available at the store. The store also featured an alterations department with expert fitters and equipment.

These Herbst models are posed on the front steps of the Fargo Federal Building, showing the fall ready-to-wear fashions from about 1940. At this time, a more utilitarian look was the style, with tailored suits, fuller skirts, hats, and furs. The women appear to be ready to take on the cool autumn days that Fargo is known for.

This female model is standing on the catwalk at the Herbst Christmas fashion show and banquet held at the Fargo Country Club in 1968. Brand names "make all the difference in the world" according to general-merchandising manager Juanita Phillips in a 1963 newspaper article. Curtsy Coats, Bettijean, Lassie Maid, and Frank Gallant were some of the coat manufacturers used by the store.

Bridal fashion shows were a big draw, especially for the bride-to-be. This model, dressed in an early 1970s bridesmaid dress, does a spin on the runway set up in the Herbst showroom. The light floral-print fabric likely drew an interest from spring wedding planners.

This model takes her turn on the catwalk showcasing a wedding dress from the Herbst Department Store bridal department. In the background, the master of ceremonies reads a statement describing the dress from her cue cards. Bill Levkoff, Mori Lee, Portrait Bridal, Bridallure, Elegant Bridal, and Biljoy were some of the wedding design brands found at Herbst.

Of course, the wedding dress was the main attraction at these bridal fashion shows. Mothers and daughters would crowd into Herbst to see the latest dress styles. This particular show took place in the early 1970s on the main showroom floor.

Mid-1970s fashions are on display in this photograph of the Herbst teenage fashion board posed in Lindenwood Park. The style at the time incorporated flare-leg jeans and pants with brightly colored patterns, often made out of Dacron polyester, nylon, and cotton blends.

Herbst Department Store won various advertising awards through the years. Some of the awards were presented by the Brand Names Foundation, *Seventeen* magazine, Retail Advertising Conference, and the Fargo-Moorhead Advertising Club. This photographer is doing a shoot next to the Red River, likely for an advertisement in the late 1970s.

This late 1970s Herbst model is dressed up for a night out on the town. Her disco-style halter-top pantsuit complete with bell bottom pants and platform shoes was quite a change from the conservative 1950s and 1960s fashions. In the late 1970s, models were hired through the Academie Agencie operated by Caroline Melroe.

This Herbst model from a late 1970s photo shoot is posing with the Henrik Wergeland statue in Island Park. The statue by Gustav Vigeland of Norway has been in the park since it was dedicated in 1908 to honor the region's Norwegian heritage. The model appears to be enjoying a beautiful day in the park, dressed in her stylish Herbst outfit.

On September 2, 1969, a Women's Day sale was held, and 12 female employees were selected to run the store for the day by their fellow employees in a storewide campaign. They were to be identified by their "friendly smiles and large pink buttons" according to the *Forum* newspaper advertisement.

Leading up to the Women's Day sale, a group of female customers were named to a merchandise-review panel. The Herbst buyers worked to identify the most wanted items and presented them to the panel for their approval. The event was touted as the "Greatest One-Day Sale Ever Held!"

The Women's Day sale featured a number of prizes during the event. Every hour, on the hour, surprise specials were announced over the intercom system, double S&H Green stamps were offered, and the grand prize of a $100 paid-up charge account was given away. The male employees served free cookies and coffee for the day.

A large number of shoppers took advantage of discounted merchandise during the Herbst fire sale in early February 1974. A month earlier, the store had suffered smoke and water damage from a fire. The sale was an opportunity to sell some of the salvageable merchandise from areas of the store not involved in the fire.

The late 1970s and early 1980s marked a difficult period for downtown Fargo businesses. The period was plagued by a slow economy, and as business left downtown, it became less of a destination for Fargo shoppers. On October 30, 1981, it was announced that the store was going out of business.

Towards the end, the store became dependent on promotional sales. Bob Herbst stated in a *Forum* article, "I thought that Penney's could go and we could still stay. That didn't turn out to be true. We could generate traffic downtown—but only if we gave something away." Here shoppers are lined up at the front doors for the going-out-of-business sale.

The going-out-of-business sale took place in early February 1982. Bargain hunters flooded the store to fill up on the discounted merchandise. By February 15, there was not much left. Auctioneers and workmen had sold or removed most evidence that this was once one of Fargo's grandest department stores, thus ending 90 years of business.

Six

The Window Displays

The North Dakota Agricultural College (later North Dakota State University) in Fargo and the University of North Dakota in Grand Forks have had a long-standing rivalry since the 1890s. This display case, featuring memorabilia from about 1923 to 1929, highlights the rivalry. On the left, a sign shows the Bison mascot of the NDAC, while on the right, another displays the Flickertail mascot of UND. The Flickertails later became the Fighting Sioux.

In 1928, the Herbst Department Store was the only place in Fargo that sold Majestic radios. On the left is the Model 71, which sold for $137.50. The Model 72 on the right sold for $167.50. An advertisement that ran in the *Forum* promoted the ability to hear the Herbert Hoover and Alfred E. Smith debates during the 1928 presidential elections.

This display was from the spring show of 1928. The theme was Art Moderne, and featured imported mannequins dressed in pink and white apparel from the era. The backdrop was designed in modernistic patterns of lavender, silver, and gray. The ornate novelty bowl on the stand held live goldfish. The display was designed by Jacob Pollari, display manager.

This display case from the April 1928 spring-themed series highlights store credit. The sign in front of the mannequin exclaims, "Credit is the Axis on which the Commercial World Revolves." The sign in the background mentions, "Credit makes the 'Easter Parade' possible. If all were obliged to outfit themselves on a cash basis the Easter Parade would be very much curtailed."

The Fargo Lodge of the Benevolent and Protective Order of Elks was organized in 1893. This display, from the 1920s or 1930s, honors the group by mounting an elk head in front of the BPOE clock symbol. The mannequin stands on top of a rug with the BPOE symbol as well. The Herbst men were active members of the order.

This display case shows everything a young fashionable couple would need to go on their honeymoon in the late 1920s and early 1930s. The couple would need trunks and fashionable outfits before they boarded a train from the Northern Pacific Railway to travel to their honeymoon destination.

Despite still being summer, an August fur sale makes sense in Fargo, where the weather turns chilly in September and it can start snowing in October. A fur coat cost between $50 and $200 in the late 1920s, depending on the kind of fur used. Wolf fur was cheaper, with squirrel, opossum, and beaver being more expensive. A coat made of muskrat or caracul lamb was the most expensive.

For this spring 1928 event, a second pair of hose could be purchased for only 10¢. To show how sturdy and strong these hose where, the swinging bench that the mannequin is sitting on is suspended by two pairs of hose.

This display from 1928 claims that the "ideal Valentine gift" was hosiery. The window dresser created a heart-shaped box that contains "candy" stockings. Onyx Pointex Chiffon and Service Hose were on sale for $1.95 to $2 a pair.

This creative display makes it appear that bolts of fabric are the results of roman candles, such as the one held by the mannequin. Eye-catching displays such as this were designed to stop pedestrians as they passed the window, drawing them into the store to find the merchandise on display, and perhaps other unexpected items.

Wool blankets are a must-have for any Fargoan. In the late 1920s or 1930s, a hut was built in the display case made of wool blankets made by the Nashua Manufacturing Company. This company was founded in Nashua, New Hampshire, in 1823 and made textiles until 1945.

This 1931 image shows the entire breadth of display windows at the Herbst Department Store. This nighttime view focuses on the brilliant lights that entice pedestrians to see what the store had for sale during the 39th anniversary celebration.

This photograph shows yet another clever display of hosiery in May 1934. The Washington Maid brand of hosiery packaging features a woman dressed in Colonial-style garments, as seen on the mannequin. Herbst employees wore similar dresses for an in-store sale promotion.

Wide-brim hats were in style in April 1940, selling for $1.95. The window display cases were renovated sometime in the late 1930s to create a more sleek and contemporary look. The merchandise for sale in the millinery department was leased by the Consolidated Millinery Company.

In honor of the Herbst Department Store's 50th anniversary, in 1942, a set of mannequins wearing fashions from the last 50 years based on *Saturday Evening Post* covers made for exciting display windows. The mannequin in this display window wears a bathing suit from 1922. The exhibit traveled around the United States and was created by fashion designer Helen Virginia Meyer.

In this display case from the *Saturday Evening Post* costume collection, a mannequin is dressed as a Red Cross nurse from World War I. Other images in the display case show nurses serving during wartime. Other *Saturday Evening Post* covers that feature wartime nursing complete the display.

The Herbst family and employees were civic minded and assisted in the war effort by having war bond drives and writing letters to soldiers. In July 1942, letters and cards from soldiers acknowledging packages sent to them in January by the Herbst Department Store were neatly arranged on a board.

During World War II, women had to go without nylon stockings, since nylon was used exclusively for war materials such as parachutes and rope. Rayon was a poor substitute, but the Herbst Department Store valiantly tried to convince customers that rayon stockings were just as good. A contest was held to see if women could tell the difference between nylon, rayon, and silk stockings, the winner receiving a $1 war stamp.

This wedding dress was designed by William Cahill, who designed bombers for Lockheed during World War II. After the war, he was aware that there would be a large market for returning soldiers getting married; thus, he took up designing wedding dresses. The discerning Fargo bride had the Herbst Department Store to thank for access to beautiful dresses designed by Cahill in Beverly Hills.

This set of matching pajamas for the whole family was made by Munsingwear, a Minneapolis-based brand. The company was famed for producing golf shirts with penguin logos. In front of the mannequins are Max Factor products, including the "Busy Man's Bar." This product included aftershave lotion, cream hair dressing, and cologne.

These mannequins appear to be cleaning up scraps of paper and placing the garbage into a trash bin as they wear dirty green, the fashionable color for fall 1959. The visual merchandiser would choose the color of clothing to promote based on what was mentioned in *Women's Wear Daily*, *Vogue*, and *Harper's Bazaar.* (Courtesy of Byron Bergman.)

Great effort was put into making exciting displays to draw attention. In May 1963, the store windows were removed to allow a car to be driven into the display case to promote Nelly Don housedresses. This display also mentions Six Flags, which was founded in Texas in 1961. (Courtesy of Byron Bergman.)

During the summer in the mid-1960s, the Herbst Department Store opened a camera shop, which actually consisted of only one small counter. Three of the four mannequins here have cameras. A reflection of cars and the photographer can be seen on the window.

As a part of the Herbst Department Store's diamond jubilee 75th anniversary in 1967, the first locomotive of the Northern Pacific Railroad was put on display at the Northern Pacific siding off of Broadway. The locomotive was built in 1870 and was called the *Minnetonka*. A pictorial history of the Northern Pacific was placed in a display window.

These stylish outfits from the early or mid-1970s probably came from the Lion's Den, the young men's clothing department. The sign in front of the shelf says "mix it up & mix it on," promoting the versatility of men's sweaters for sale.

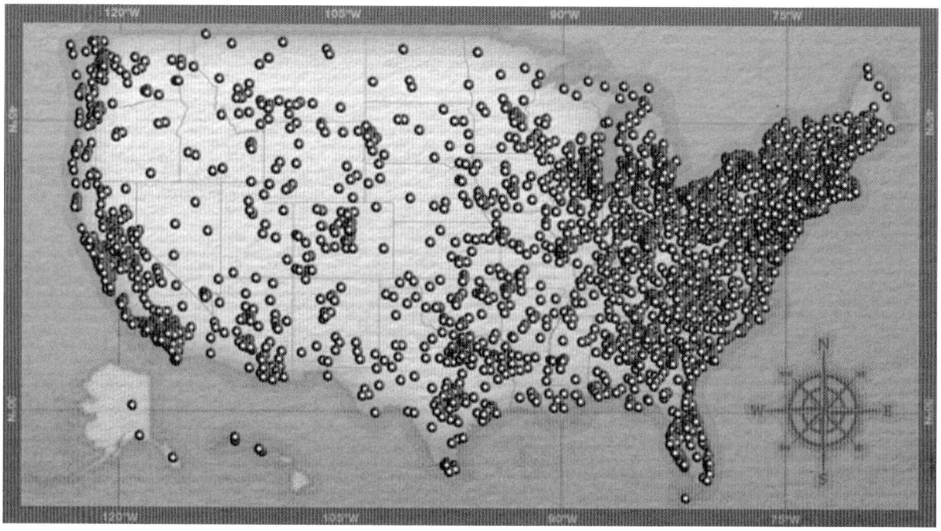